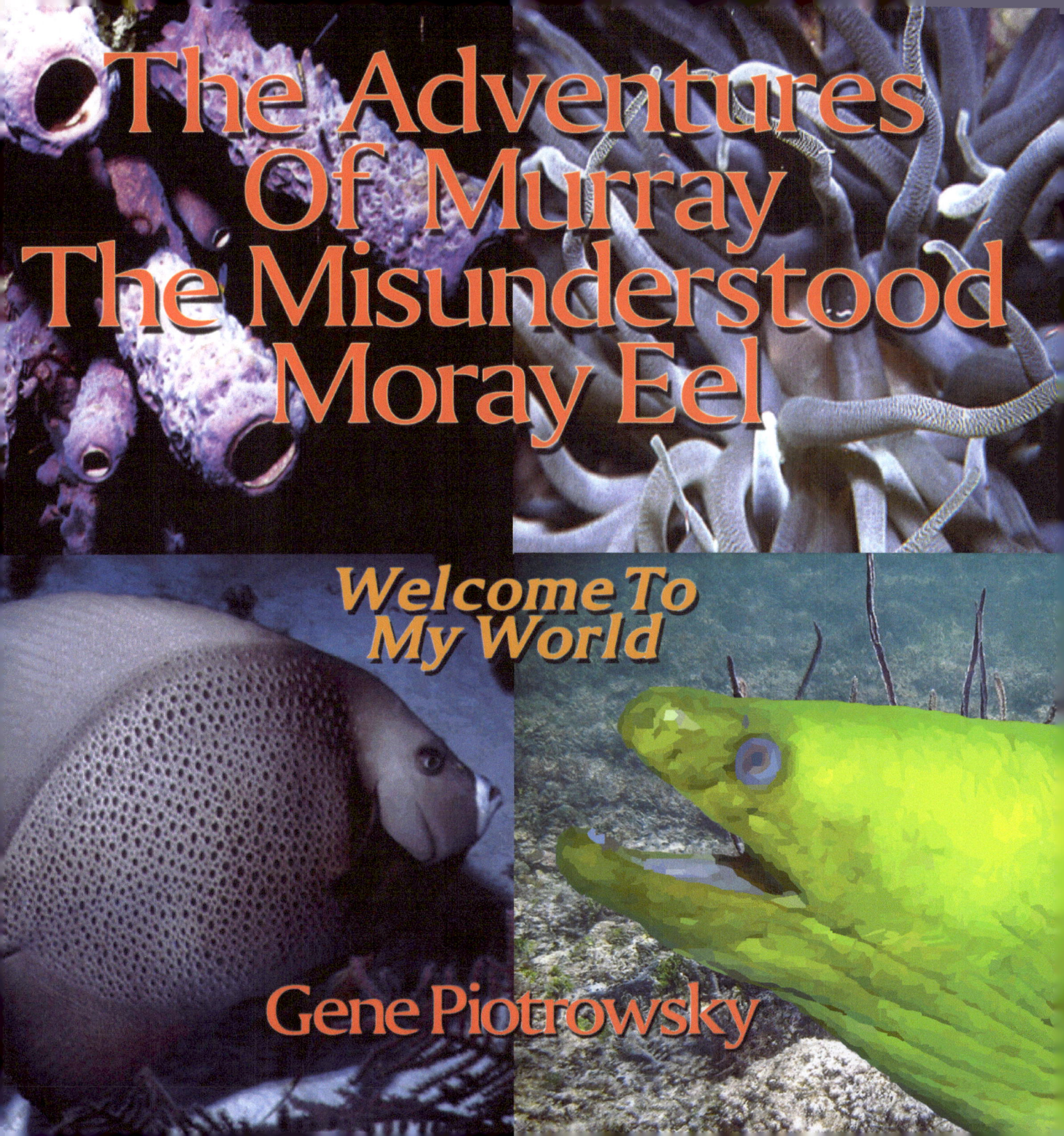

The Adventures Of Murray The Misunderstood Moray Eel

Welcome To My World

Gene Piotrowsky

The Adventures Of Murray The Misunderstood Moray Eel

Welcome To My World

Published by CheshireKids Entertainment
15900 SW 95 Avenue, No. 208 South Miami, FL 33157

Library of Congress Cataloging-in-Publication Data
Piotrowsky, Gene
ISBN 978-1489505668

Tags - Moray Eels for Children -Underwater Photography - Children - Education

Book Design by Gene Piotrowsky

To Kim,
The Love Of My Life.

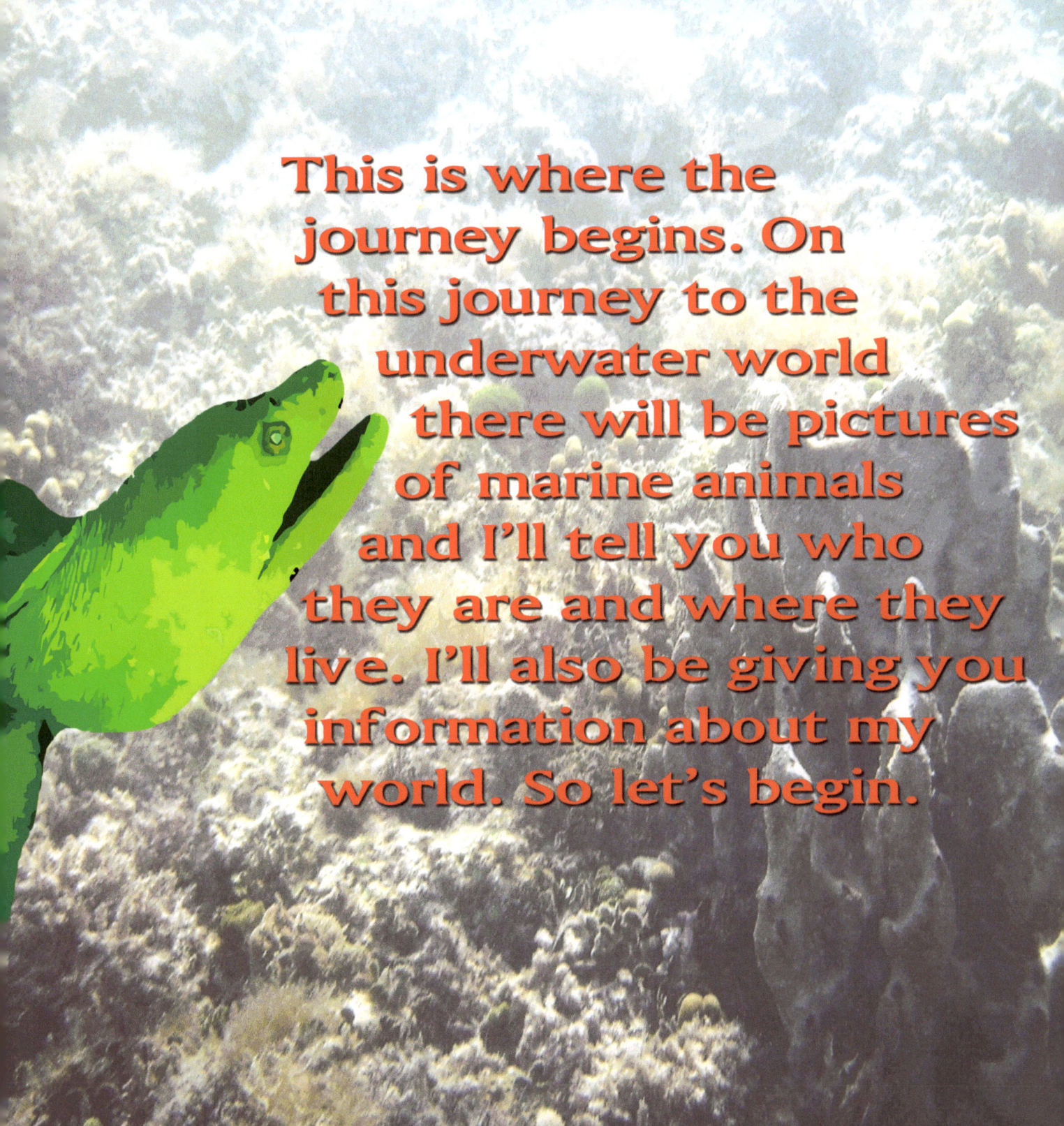

This is where the journey begins. On this journey to the underwater world there will be pictures of marine animals and I'll tell you who they are and where they live. I'll also be giving you information about my world. So let's begin.

The average depth
of the ocean is
12,000 feet -
the deepest part
is 36,198 feet in
the Mariana Trench
in the western Pacific.

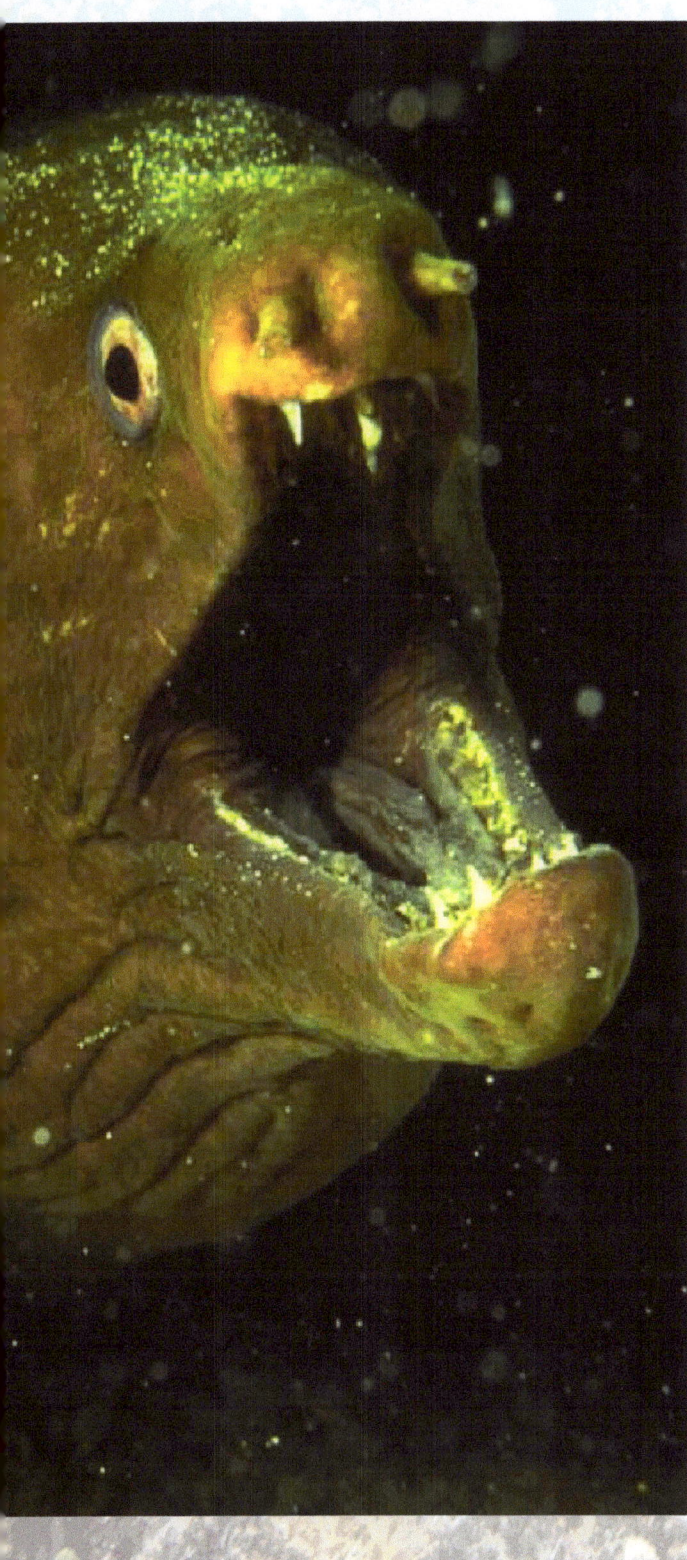

This Is My World

There you are. I was wondering when you would open this page. Now that you're here I want to introduce myself and my underwater world. I'm Murray and I'm a Green Moray Eel. Didn't you see the cover with my name in lights? First let me say, we morays have been getting a really bad rap. We're always accused about being vicious, always shown with our mouths open like Bernie over there. Well here's the truth about that. In order for us to get oxygen from the water we have to continuously keep our mouths opening and closing to pump water through our gills. We Green Morays are big usually about 6 feet long. There was one of us who ate too much and got to 8 feet long. We're usually found living in coral reefs or rocky shorelines. It's sometimes dangerous out there and we find a nice hole in the reef. We just sit there sometimes waiting for a meal to swim by. Moray's hunt for food at night. We really don't have very good eyesight so we find our food by smell. We love fish, crabs, squid and shrimp, my favorite. Green Morays live along the waters of the Western Atlantic Ocean. We're all over from New Jersey all along the coast down to the Caribbean Sea, throughout all the Caribbean Islands, even as far south as Brazil. Some of us live in Bermuda and even in the Gulf of Mexico. Just remember, when you are visiting my world, please don't stick your hand into any hole, that may be our home.

The oceans make up 70% of the Earth's surface - but we know very little about them.

It's All In My Family

Moray eels are all over the oceans of the world. There are about 19 of my moray relatives, all very different looking living in the Western Atlantic Ocean, the Caribbean Sea all the way down to Central America and South America. In fact there are two morays that are also found in other oceans as well. The Redface Eel is found in the Pacific Ocean and the Indian Ocean and the other moray is the Broadbanded Moray which possibly is found in the Pacific Ocean. Look at the two photos over here. The top photo is of a Spotted Moray. They are medium size morays and they grow to about 3 feet long. They are the most common morays that snorkelers and divers see. They are usually seen with their heads poking out of their holes in the reef. Unlike me, they are more active during the day feeding on crustaceans, such as crabs, shrimps, and lobsters, this is making me hungry, and of course fish. The bottom photo is of an Ocellated Moray. It's a small moray, it usually grows to about 1 foot. Like most morays it also has poor eyesight, but it has a very good sense of smell. Of course at night in the ocean there is no light, so all nocturnal animals use the sense of smell to find food. But enough of me and my family. Now it's time to show you some more of my underwater world.

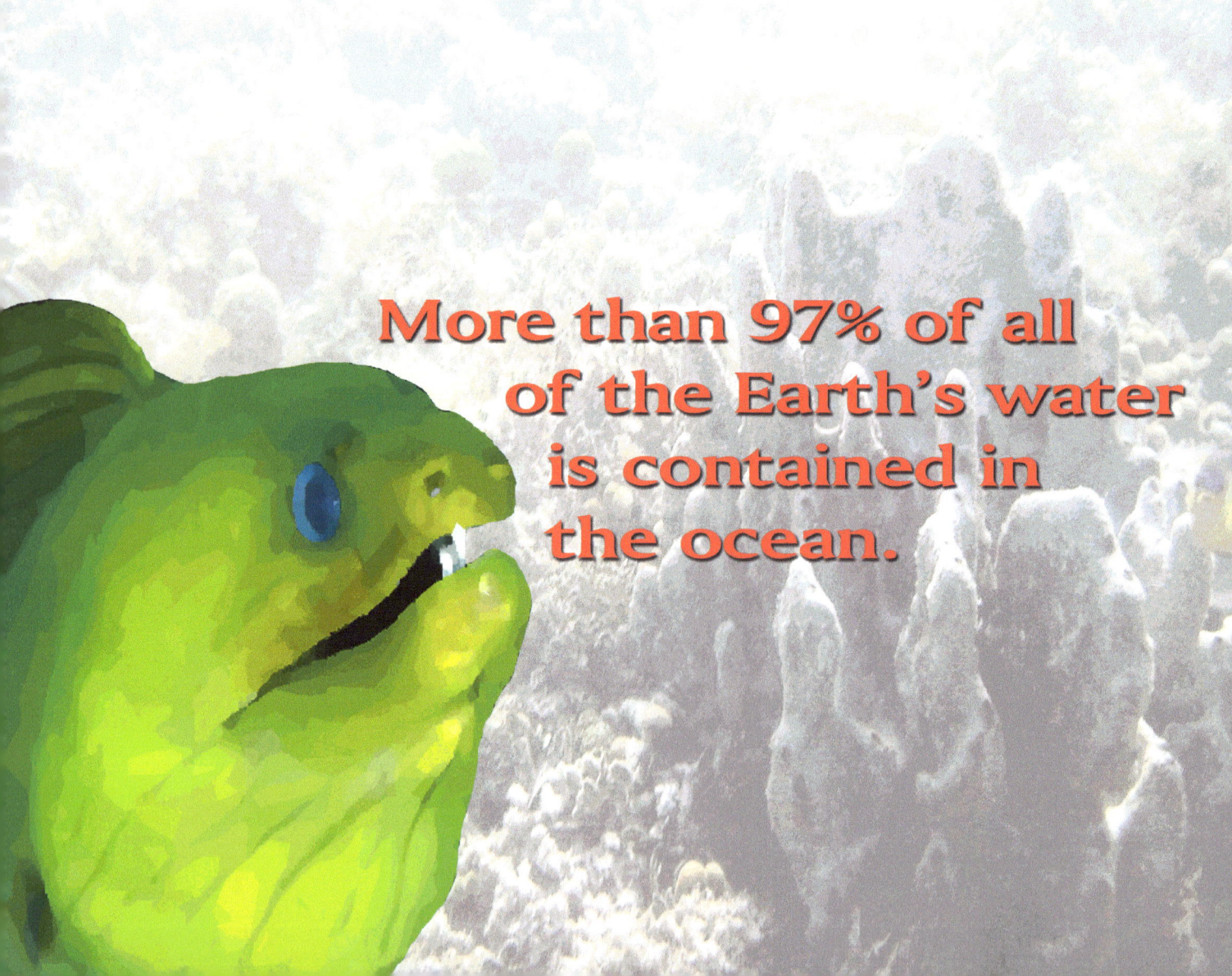

More than 97% of all
of the Earth's water
is contained in
the ocean.

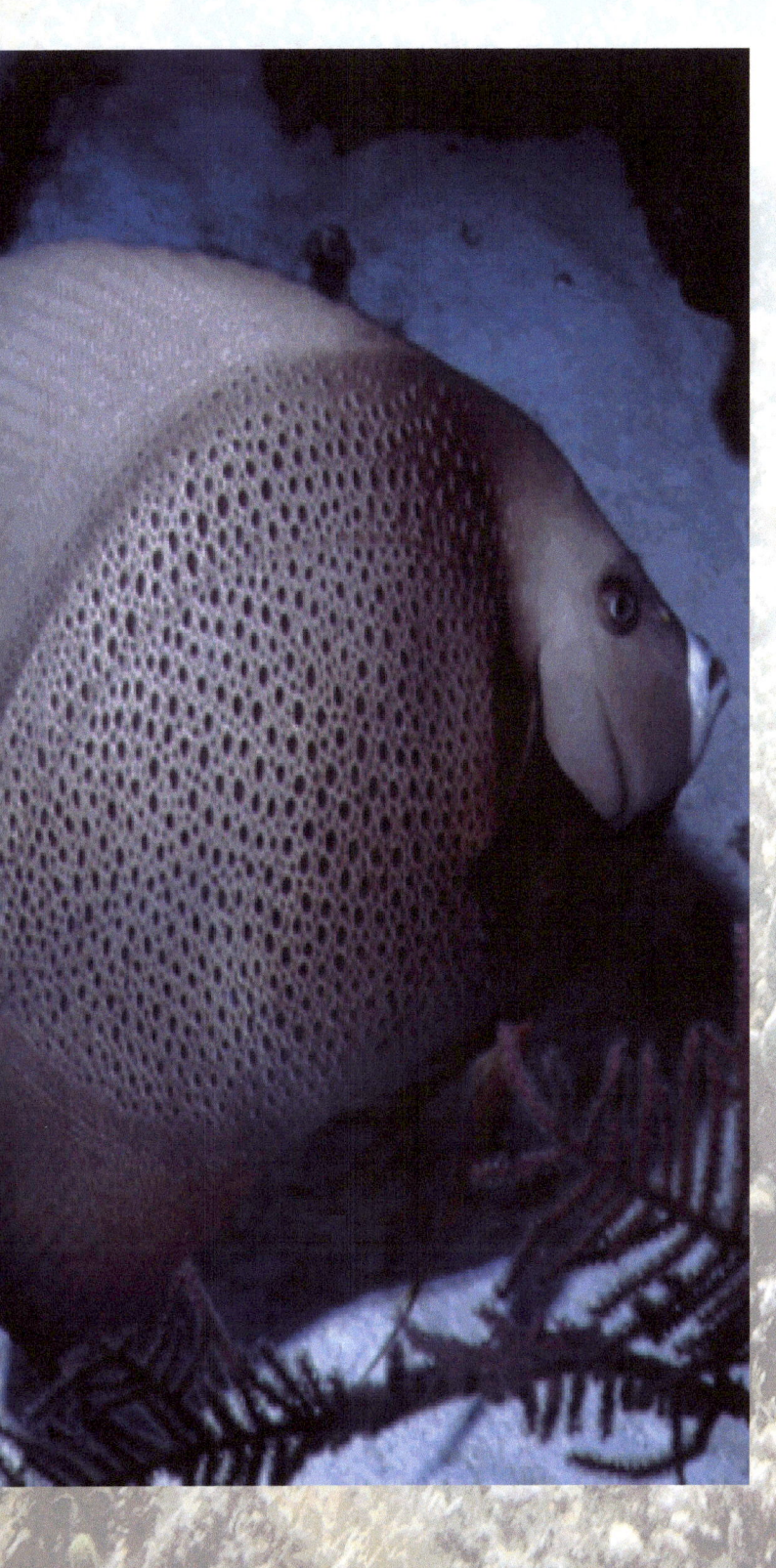

Our Angels - The Gray Angelfish

Now that we are finished with eels I want to tell you about Angelfish. They are some of the most beautiful fish in the ocean. There are about 74 different kinds of angelfish and 7 of these in the Western Atlantic Ocean and Caribbean Sea. I am going to show you 3 angelfish that I think are my favorites, favorites to look at, not necessarily to eat. The angelfish on this page is the Gray Angelfish. They are large fish, when they are full grown their size is from 10 inches to 24 inches long. They live on the same coral reef mostly by themselves. They are more common than some of the other angelfish and are easily approachable, which is good when you're snorkeling or diving. Their diet is mostly sea sponges, coral and sea animals, but they also eat algae and sea grasses.
Now to the next angelfish, the French Angelfish.

It is estimated that there are between 500,000 and 5,000,000 marine species not yet discovered.

Our Angels - The French Angelfish

You can see from this photo how striking the French Angelfish is. The scales are black with yellow rims and the face becomes light blue with a white chin and mouth. The French Angelfish like the Gray Angelfish grow to about the same size, 13.5" to 14" long. Unlike the Gray Angelfish the French Angelfish are often seen in pairs and remain with the same mate throughout their lives. Together they move around the coral reefs during the day, and seek a safe place for the night. They are also very territorial, but they are very curious and will not shy away from divers. They are also found in the Western Atlantic Ocean. You can find them from Florida to the Bahamas, the Caribbean Sea and all the way down to Brazil. They are also found in the Gulf of Mexico and in the Eastern Atlantic Ocean. As young angels they serve as cleaners like cleaner gobies, wrasses and shrimp, but this usually stops when they grow larger. We'll get into cleaners later. But for now these cleaner fish remove parasites from larger fish. The French Angelfish are omnivorous, they eat sponges,algae as well as corals.

98% of the ocean floor has not yet been discovered.

Our Angels - The Queen Angelfish

Queen Angelfish are absolutely beautiful as you can see in this photograph. The coloring from the bluish body to the black spot on the forehead and the spots of electric blue surrounded by a narrow electric blue ring to the yellow tail. The Queen Angelfish size is very similar to the Gray Angelfish and the French Angelfish, about 12" and a little bigger. The Queen Angelfish also lives on coral reefs, but some fish live alone or in pairs. Like their cousins they can be found in the Western Atlantic Ocean, down through the Caribbean Sea to South America. They are also a popular aquarium fish and have been used as a food fish, I wasn't talking about me, but there have been reports of ciguatera poisoning. This means that the flesh can be toxic to humans. They eat mostly sponges and coral. This ends the Angelfish section.

Water pressure at the deepest point in the ocean is more than 8 tons per square inch, the same as one person trying to hold up 50 jumbo jets.

Anemones

Sea Anemones look like some dangerous alien animals with many tentacles, but are only dangerous to the small fish or small bits of food that float past them. Anemones are predatory marine animals which are related to corals and jellyfish. Sea Anemones attach themselves to the bottom of the coral reef by an adhesive foot, called a basal disc. They range in size from 1 inch to over 6 feet. At the end of each tentacle are stingers that when the food touches it, they automatically trigger and launch a harpoon-like structure that attaches to the organism, injects a dose of venom into the prey. Don't worry, humans are not in any danger. As you can see in the upper photo the ends of the tentacles and the small bits of food that pass their way. There are many varieties, each different in size and color.

The octopus's speed of travel never exceeds that of the surrounding waves.

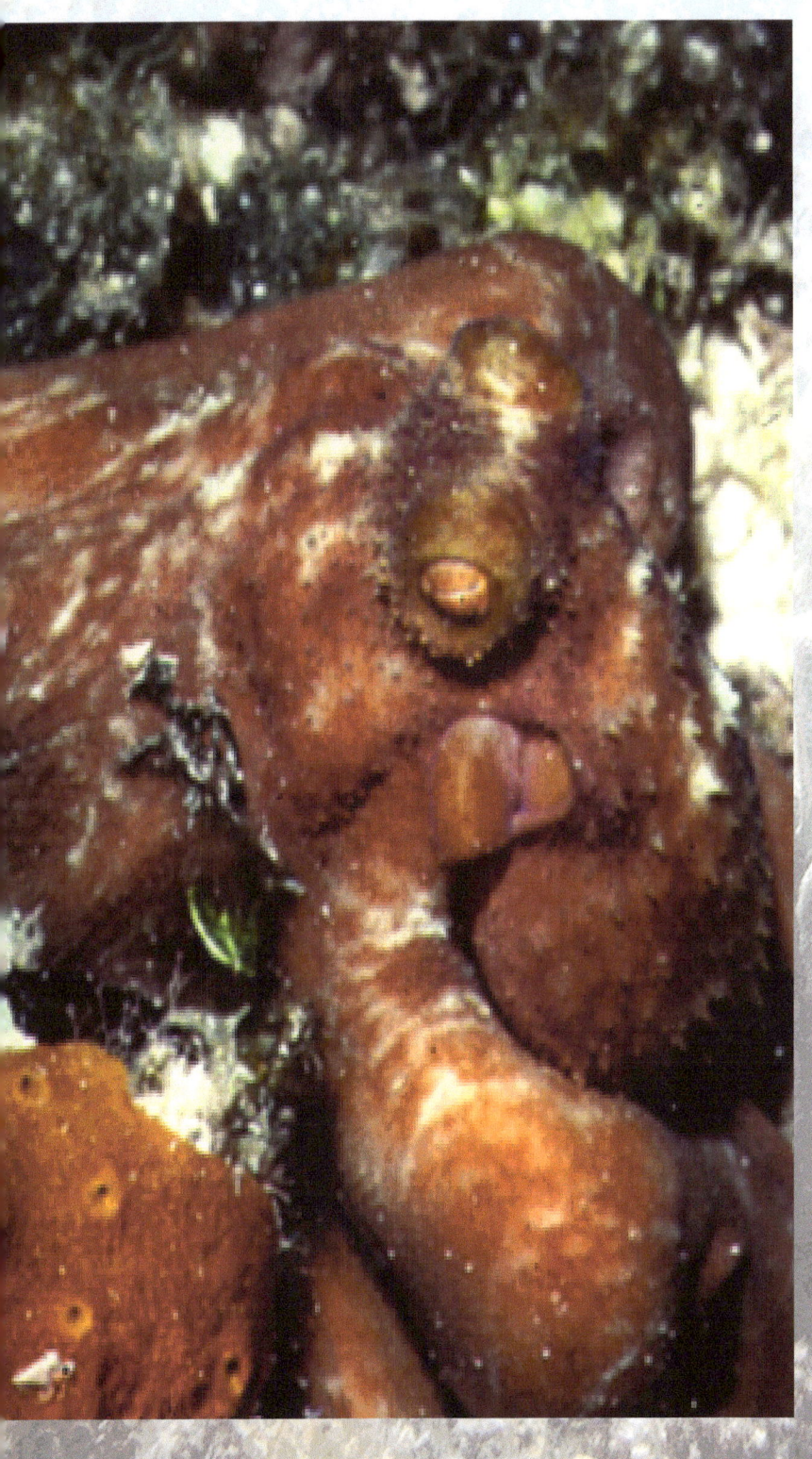

Octopus

Here is probably one of the most intelligent and inquisitive animals in the sea. They are actually referred to as cephalopods. They are related to squids, cuttlefish and nautilus. Octopus have eight arms, with a hard beak, like a parrots beak, with its mouth at the center of the arms. One of the most unique features about the Octopus is that when frightened they can hide by changing their body color to match their surroundings as well as changing the appearance of their skin to also match their surroundings. Of course when they really get annoyed their color changes to red like in this photo. They can also squirt black ink to confuse their predators. Octopus move about by expelling a jet of water. Or if not in danger just crawling over the ocean bottom. They show great skill at problem solving.

Salt in the oceans and seas comes from rocks that have been broken and worn down by the wind and water. Chemicals from the rocks dissolve in the water and make it salty.

Divers In My World - Feeding Fish

As you can see my world is continuously being invaded by people. They love to explore the reefs and wrecks, and they think we're undernourished so they bring food with them. Here's a diver who just sounded the dinner bell by opening his bag of food. He's surrounded by Sergeant Majors fish, they're the ones with the stripes. They are small about 8 inches long. Sergeant Majors are found all over the Caribbean, Gulf of Mexico and all the way to South America. The other fish with the yellow stripe is the Yellowtail Snapper. They are bigger, grow to about 28 inches and found throughout the Caribbean Sea. I just wish the divers would bring down some really good eats. The last one brought down salami. Please give me a break.

There are about 4,000 coral reef fish species worldwide.

Divers In My World - Groupers

Divers love to swim with large fish like this Nassau Grouper. The Nassau Grouper is one of the larger reef fish attaining a length up to over 3 feet. Unfortunately they have suffered a dramatic decline due to over-fishing. What is interesting is that individuals are capable of changing their color pattern to resemble their surrounding environment. They usually live on coral reefs or other hard bottoms at a depth of 300 feet. Like all the fish in this book they are found throughout the Bahamas, Florida, Gulf of Mexico and the Caribbean. They eat fish and are found visiting cleaning stations to get rid of parasites. They are classified as an endangered species.

Tropical coral reefs
border the shores
of 109 countries.

Divers In My World - Soft Coral

There are many varieties of corals in the ocean. We have the hard corals and the soft corals. I better explain what a coral is. Corals are small animals. They build homes, what we call reefs, by secreting calcium which builds up through hundreds of years. These reefs look like rock, but are the homes of thousands of tiny animals who come out at night to feed on the food that passes by. Besides the corals that are reefs and what we call hard corals, there are soft corals that resemble plants. They have a whip look and they sway in the ocean current. The diver on top of this photo is shown through what looks like a jungle of soft corals. Coral reefs and soft corals are very important to the life of a healthy ocean and have to be protected.

Coral reefs are made by millions of small sea animals. When they die, their skeletons are left behind and this forms a reef slowly - slowly.

Another Look At Soft Corals

Corals come in so many shapes and colors. Some look like lifeless rocks without any coloration. Some look like plants with beautiful shapes and colors, but they have one common feature in that they are created by coral polyps, very small animals that build the coral reefs and the soft corals that they live in. The photo of this beautiful, colorful and graceful looking coral is a colony of hundreds or thousands of these tiny animals. They come out mostly at night and wait for food to pass them and then catch it. Unlike hard corals, soft corals do not build reefs, but may live on them. In the photo the polyps are half out of their protective homes waiting for a passing meal. The white specs in the water are passing plankton or other small organisms. Corals are found in the tropical parts of the Atlantic and Pacific Oceans.

Coral reefs cover about 1/15th of the ocean floor. About 1/4 of all marine species make reefs their home.

A Coral Home

Coral reefs built by hard corals are the homes of many of the oceans' animals. I myself have a very cosy hole in a reef. This is a photo of a Squirrelfish that has made this hole in the reef its home. As you can see they have very large eyes and are usually red in color. They are common on most reefs and are primarily nocturnal which means that they are active at night. That's why their eyes are so large. At night they roam the sandy bottom and the sea grass beds feeding on small crustaceans. Crustaceans are shrimp and crabs. The Squirrelfish is not very big with their total length reaching about 12 inches. They have lots of relatives, about 65 of them. They include other types of Squirrelfish and very similar looking Soldierfish. All these fish are found in the Caribbean Sea all the way down to South America and Central America. Some are found as far north as Bermuda and into the Gulf of Mexico.

Coral reefs make up less than 1/2% of the ocean floor.

A Sponge A-Frame Home

This home is made up of sponges. Not the kind you may use in your home, although before there were man-made sponges, the sponges used for bathing were from the sea. Sponges come in a wide variety of shapes and colors. All sponges are animals. They get oxygen and the food they need by a constant flow of water through their bodies which also removes waste products. Many sponges because of their shapes make wonderful homes. This Royal Gramma fish found a perfect A-frame home. Royal Gramma fish belong to the basslets family. The Royal Gramma is a very colorful fish. The front part is purple, which looks blue underwater, with the rest of the fish a bright orange-yellow. The Royal Gramma grows to about 3 and 1/8 inches. It's found throughout the Caribbean Sea.

It is estimated that more than 90% of marine species are directly or indirectly dependent on the reefs.

Small Purple Tube Sponges

I said that there are so many kinds of sponges in the ocean. Here we have Purple Tube Sponges. Purple Tube Sponges come in different sizes and they grow in different ways. These sponges are growing on the side of a coral reef that is on the edge of a very deep trench. In the Caribbean Sea some of the islands were formed from extinct volcanos so the surrounding water is very deep. As you can see they attract a lot of little fish that use the sponge for homes or find food near them. On the page before, we talked about how sponges get their oxygen and food from water passing through their bodies. In the Pacific along the Great Barrier Reef some sponges there produce up to 3 times more oxygen than they can use, which helps the reefs. The sponges in the Caribbean don't produce the same amount of oxygen for their reefs.

The Great Barrier Reef
in Australia is
1,243 miles long.
It is the largest
living structure
on Earth.

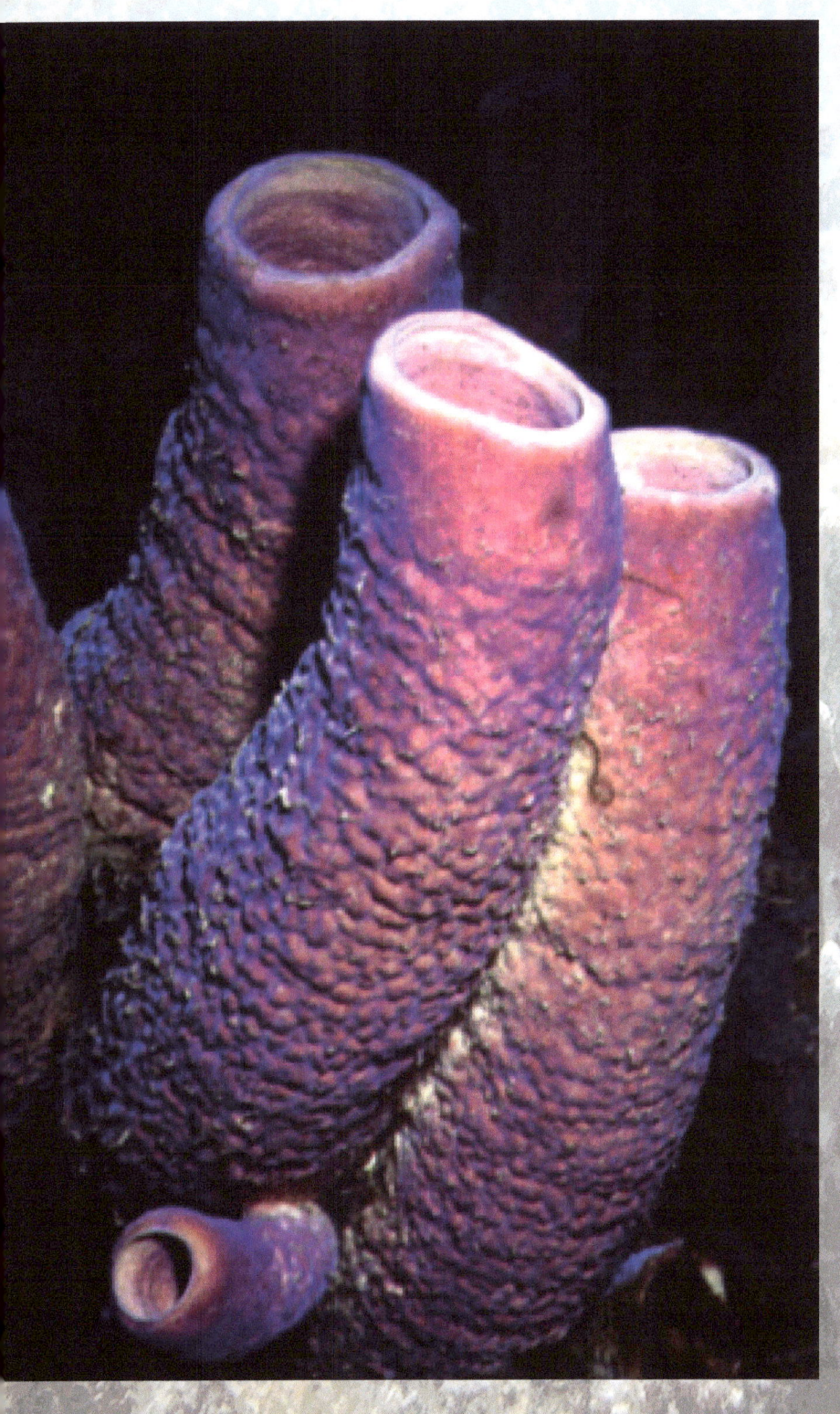

Large Purple Tube Sponges

I know what you are saying, oh no, Murray has another photo of Purple Tube Sponges. OK this is going to be the last of the sponges. I wanted you to see the difference of how these sponges grow. These Purple Tube Sponges are much larger than on the page before. They are also growing up on the coral reef. If you look closely between the two Tube Sponges on the right you can see the arms of a Brittle Star sticking out. Sponges are one of the favorite places for Brittle Stars to call home. They are related to Sea Stars or as they are sometimes called Starfish. They move about the reef in a swimming motion. Most Brittle Stars have 5 arms. Because they are so tiny they feed on bacteria and microalgae. They are found throughout the Caribbean Sea, Central America and South America.

The Atlantic Ocean is the youngest of all the oceans.
The Atlantic Ocean is the world's saltiest ocean.

A Rock Hind Searches The Reef

The Rock Hind is part of the Sea Bass family and they are related to the Groupers. You can see the same type of jaw that the Nassau Grouper had in the Grouper Diver page. The Rock Hind is not a big fish only reaching about 2 feet in length. In the Grouper family the Hind would be medium. They live by themselves on the reefs and they feed on crabs and fish. This is very interesting. They draw their food into their gullet, or throat by a powerful suction which is created when they open their large mouths. I'm going to throw something new at you. Groupers are hermaphroditic. Don't freak out, all this means is that they start their lives as females, but they change to males with maturity, when they grow up. You'll find this is common among fish in my ocean world.

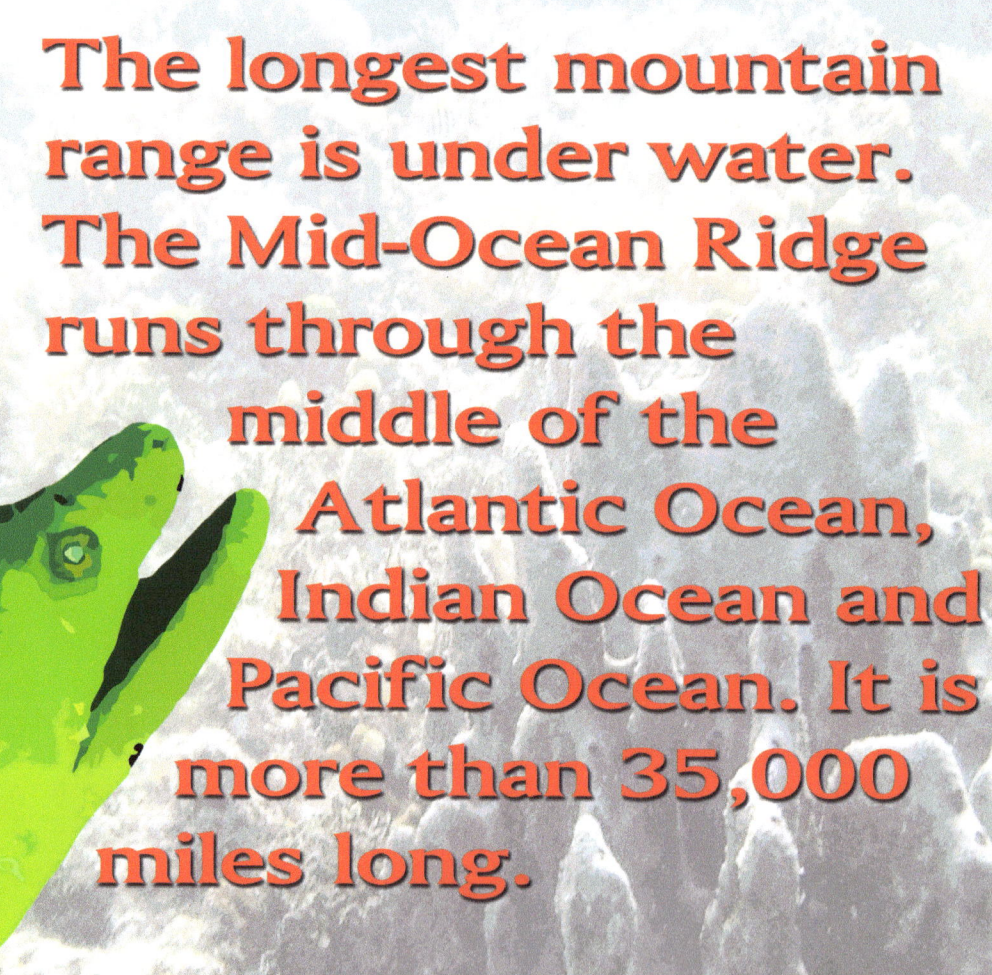

The longest mountain range is under water. The Mid-Ocean Ridge runs through the middle of the Atlantic Ocean, Indian Ocean and Pacific Ocean. It is more than 35,000 miles long.

Cleaning Stations

This is my favorite topic in my sea world. We have cleaning stations set-up all over the ocean. Here's what happens in them. Large fish like the Grouper over here pick up parasites during their travels. Parasites are a form of life that, in this case live and feed on the Grouper. Now they can't get rid of them by themselves. So they visit a Cleaning Station. Here Cleaner Fish or sometimes Cleaner Shrimp go about eating the parasites on the Grouper while he is holding steady in this giant piece of concrete tunnel that was put on the reef by humans. So the Grouper gets his parasites taken off and the Cleaner Fish gets a meal. This is a symbiotic relationship. Each fish is getting something from each other.

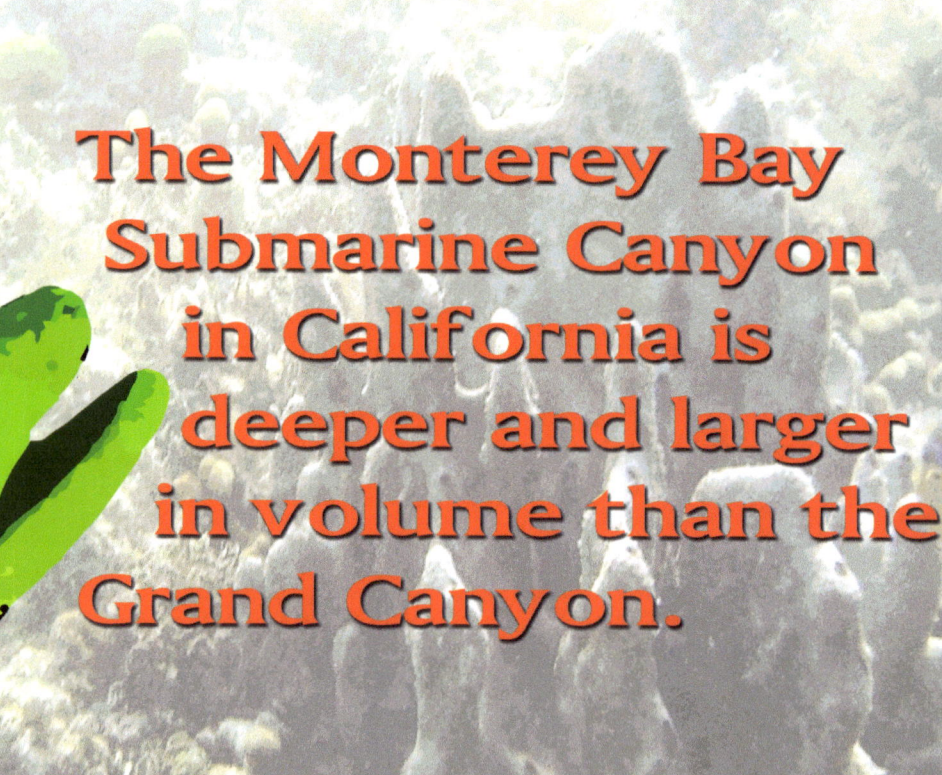

The Monterey Bay
Submarine Canyon
in California is
deeper and larger
in volume than the
Grand Canyon.

Parrotfish

Here's a beautiful Stoplight Parrotfish. These are very important fish for a healthy reef. These fish have jaws that resemble a parrot's beak. This allows the Parrotfish to grind up algae that starts to grow on the reef. They smash up the coral and eat the coral animals and then discharge the coral which is now turned to sand. If the algae was to grow on the reef it would kill the coral animals and the reef would die. Another very interesting fact about some of the Parrotfish family is that when nighttime occurs, the Parrotfish encase themselves in a transparent envelope or cocoon made of mucous secreted from an organ on their head. It's believed that the cocoon hides their scent from predators like Moray Eels. Don't get me wrong some of my best friends are Parrotfish.

Great White Sharks can go as long as three months without eating.

Inside A Ship Wreck

There are hundreds of ship wrecks in the oceans. Some have sunk by storms. Some by accidents or some by wars. Anyway all the wrecks in all the seas become reefs. Given time all kinds of animals find the wrecks and settle into a new home. Now the wrecks are created by sinking old ships in fairly shallow water to create artificial reefs. These reefs are very important to the oceans. Some reefs protect the land from storms. They also let divers explore the wrecks and they allow fisherman to find places to fish. We're looking from inside this wreck to the open sea. It doesn't look like there is a lot of life but the beams are covered with coral. To me it looks like a very inviting cave to live in. For divers the most important thing is not to get trapped inside the wreck without a way to get back out.

Using its web-like skin between its arms, an octopus can carry up to a dozen crabs back to its den.

Fish Making A Wreck A Home

Here's another wreck that clearly has become a home to coral, sponges and fish. This wreck was sunk by a hurricane during the late 1800's. It was a large ship that broke in half. One section, from amidships to the bow lies in fairly deep water. The aft, or back part of the ship was broken up and scattered over the ocean floor in shallow water. You can see the school of Blackbar Soldierfish swimming around. You can always tell if the reef is natural or man-made. The pieces covered with coral have definite straight lines. In the world above or below the water, when you look at nature you will never see straight lines. When a ship goes down and becomes a wreck the first animals are usually fish that find there way to the wreck. Coral and sponges take longer to drift toward the wreck and begin colonies. It usually takes time for a wreck to be covered with life like this one.

Lobsters are excellent swimmers and they use their fanned tails to move forward and backwards.

The Adventures Of Murray The Misunderstood Moray Eel

Welcome To My World

I guess that this is the end of our journey together. I hope that you enjoyed the trip and that I was able to pass on some facts and information about my world. I really enjoyed having you down here with me. I hope some of you will be more curious and when your are allowed, plan to visit me down here. Just remember that in order to enjoy this world you have to learn all the safety rules through the many certified diving and snorkeling organizations that teach these courses. I also hope that you see this world of beauty and wonder and think of how you can do your part in protecting this vast underwater world. I've just given you a brief look in this book, but I'll be back with another adventure and a look into a different part of my world. So look for me again in the not to distant future. There's an old saying I like to tell my new friends to the underwater world, when you do visit me down here soon.

"Take Only Pictures, Leave Only Bubbles"

Sharks never run out of teeth. If one is lost, another spins forward from the rows and rows of backup teeth.

About The Author

I first met Gene back in 1970. That's when he first visited my world. At first he just came down to see what was down here and then as I found out later he was a photographer and was bringing down underwater cameras. He was already an advertising art director and a book designer. He would visit several times a year. Living in New York and diving in the cold water never suited him, so he would come down to the Caribbean to dive and photograph. Later on he told me he started working in film and television. Of course he brought his graphic art talent with him and started designing opening title credits for television movies and shows. Gene was awarded with his first Emmy Nomination for a PBS Film, "The Gardener's Son". Later he was again nominated for another Emmy, but that was for sound mixing and editing. The show was a CBS Special "A Special Day In The Year Of The Child." He won that Emmy. Gene has been involved in series television for NBC, "True Blue", ABC, Bellevue Emergency" and "Our Home" for Lifetime as well many others. In 2003 he started writing children's books of the underwater world.Then came Hurricane Katrina, which destroyed his home and over forty years of photographs. The photos in this book are some of the very few that survived. He is now living in Miami to be close to the tropical waters and will continue to write books for young people.

www.ingramcontent.com/pod-product-compliance
Lightning Source LLC
Chambersburg PA
CBHW041514280526
45792CB00004B/1253